**W9-CEY-535**

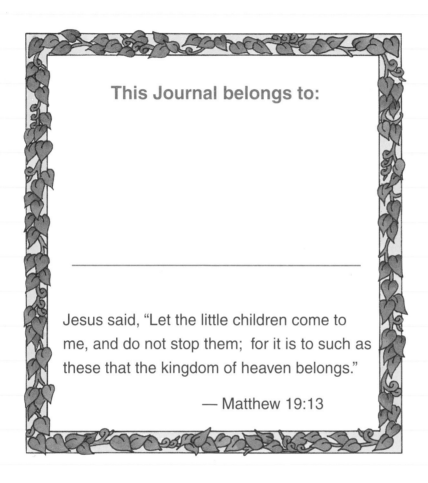

This Journal belongs to:

_____

Jesus said, "Let the little children come to me, and do not stop them; for it is to such as these that the kingdom of heaven belongs."

— Matthew 19:13

LIBRARY
St. Mark's UM Church
100 N. Highway 46 Bypass
Bloomington, IN 47408
332-5788

My Journal

A Place to Write
about God and Me

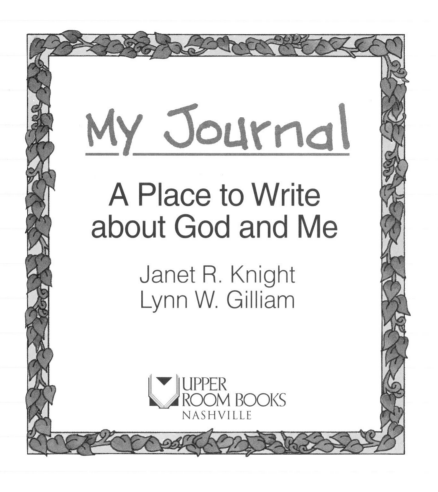

My Journal

A Place to Write about God and Me

Janet R. Knight
Lynn W. Gilliam

UPPER ROOM BOOKS
NASHVILLE

My Journal
Copyright © 1997 by The Upper Room. All rights reserved.

No part of this book may be reproduced in any manner what-
soever without written permission of the publisher except in
brief quotations embodied in critical articles or reviews. For
information address The Upper Room, 1908 Grand Avenue,
P.O. Box 189, Nashville, Tennessee 37202.

Unless otherwise noted, scripture quotations are from the *New
Revised Standard Version of the Bible,* © 1989 by the Division
of Christian Education, National Council of the Churches of
Christ in the USA, and are used by permission.

Scripture quotations designated TEV are from the *Good News
Bible, The Bible in Today's English Version — Old Testament:*
Copyright © American Bible Society 1976; New Testament:
Copyright © American Bible Society 1966, 1971, 1976.

Scripture quotations designated CEV are from the *Contemporary English Version* text. Copyright © American Bible Society
1991, 1992. Used by permission.

Design: Chris Schechner, *Schechner & Associates*
Cover illustration by Linda Simmons. Border illustrations by
Lisa Sims (February, April, May, July, September, October,
November, December); Chris Schechner (opening pages,
January, March, seasonal pages); Lynn McClain (June);
Mary Haverfield (August).
Pockets and Capp illustrations by Chris Sharp.

Printed in the United States of America
First Printing: May 1997 (10)

Table of Contents

A message to readers about My Journal

Do you know what a journal is? It's a little bit like a diary. You may already keep a diary. If you do, think about the things you write in it.

You might write about things that happen during the day, or you might write about your feelings. You might write about your friends or your family.

A journal is like a diary about you and God. In it you can write about the same kinds of things you write in your diary. The difference is that you're writing to God. Writing in your journal is almost like writing a prayer. It is one way of telling God about happy times and sad times, about worries and fears.

You can use your journal to help you to remember people you want to pray for. You can use it to say, "Thank you, God," or "I'm sorry, God."

This book is divided into months with four weeks in each month. Some months have parts of a fifth week in them. That happens about every three months. When your month has an extra week in it, turn to page 108 to find some things to think about for those extra weeks. If you have trouble knowing which week in the month a certain week is, ask a parent to number the weeks on a big calendar for you.

You don't have to begin your journal in January. You can start it any month. And you can write in your journal any time during your week. Some of you might like to have a regular time to write, like Sunday night before your school week begins. But some of you may want to write whenever you feel like it, and that's okay, too!

You might find that having a special place to write in your journal will help you to be able to think about the things you want to write. If you don't already have a quiet place at home, try to find one. A quiet place might be a very obvious place, like on your bed. Then again, it might be a kind of hidden-away place like in a tree house or a closet or under a staircase.

A quiet place can be any place where you feel comfortable and relaxed and safe, but it does need to be quiet. You might have two places — one for cold weather and one for warm weather. If you have trouble finding a quiet place in your home, ask your mom or dad to help you make one.

Each week of *My Journal* has two or three questions to help you start writing. You can write about those questions, or you can write about something else that you need to talk with God about. You might have so much to write some weeks that you need more space. If that happens, you might want to buy a notebook to use as part of your journal.

A spiral notebook is the best kind of notebook because the pages won't come out as easily, and you can lay a spiral notebook flat. That makes it easier for you to write in it. If you do use a notebook to write more for your week, be sure to write something like *Continued from February, Week 1,* or whatever week it is, at the top of the page. Then it will be easier for you to go back later and read what you wrote. Lots of people like to do that.

Using your "People (or "Things") I Want to Pray for This Week" can help you to remember when you know that someone or something has a special need for God's help. If your list is longer than you have room for here, you can continue it in your notebook, too.

You can use the prayer printed on the page, or you can make up your own prayer. You might want to pray the short prayer printed on the page at certain times each day of the week and still pray the prayer you normally pray before you go to sleep every night.

We hope that as you write in your journal, you will know that God is with you every day and that God cares about the things that you care about. Isn't that a good thing to know?

A message to parents

My *Journal* is a compilation and expansion of the regular feature of the same name that appears in *Pockets* devotional magazine for children. The intent of that feature and of this book is to introduce children to a way of communicating with God that can help them make connections between their Sunday faith and their daily life.

Most children probably make those connections more often and more easily than we adults do, for the realities of our daily lives filled with busy-ness and various stresses tend to obscure for us adults an awareness of God's constant presence with us and of God's loving activity in our lives. This characteristic of adulthood, alas, affects our children long before they reach their own adulthood. They may come into the world with a sense of awe and an ability to accept things that we adults quickly question or dismiss, but it is not long before children face their own pressures and the realities of their own daily existence. When they do, they begin to lose those characteristics of childhood that made Jesus say, "Let the little children come to me, and do not stop them; for it is to such as these that the kingdom of heaven belongs" (Matt. 19:13).

The discipline of journaling can give children a means of keeping in touch with their sense of God's presence in their lives. Journaling will not work for all children, just as it doesn't work for all adults. There are some things you as a parent can do to encourage your child to journal, but beyond doing these things parents need to let their children establish their own methods and frequency of journaling. In the end, if the child says that journaling is not for him or her, the parent needs to respect that.

My Journal is divided into months of four weeks each. For the months in which a fifth week falls, there are extra journaling exercises beginning on page 108. The weeks are undated in order to make *My Journal* usable any year. Because of that, your child may have difficulty keeping up with the weeks or with identifying fifth weeks. If you have a family calendar, you might want to number the weeks and mark the fifth weeks on that calendar.

The questions for each week are intended to give the child something to begin writing and thinking about. However, if the child has something else to write about that feels more important at the time, that is quite all right.

Here are a few things you can do to encourage your child to journal:

• Provide your child with his or her own Bible. For the purpose of *My Journal,* it is better not to have a children's Bible, because these Bibles often omit sections of scripture. Choose a modern translation for your child. Most of the quoted scripture in *My Journal* is from the New Revised Standard Version (NRSV) of the Bible. For consistency you might want to choose that version for your child's own Bible. However, other versions, such as the Today's English (TEV), the New International (NIV), and the Contemporary English (CEV) are good. It is probably better to start with a version other than the King James. Although very beautiful, the King James Version is difficult for children to read and to understand.

• Help your child know how to use the Bible. Explain about the two Testaments, show them the Table of Contents, and help them to understand chapter and verse designations.

• Help your child find a quiet place for journaling, praying, and Bible reading. If your child has a room of his or her own, you might want to help create a special corner in that room. For children who don't have their own room, you might help them find a place in the house where they can be relatively quiet and undisturbed. Explain to other family members that when your child is in that place he or she needs to be left undisturbed.

• Your child may need more writing room than the pages in this book allow. Help your child choose a notebook to use as a supplement to *My Journal.* A spiral notebook works well, since the pages will lay flat and won't come out easily.

We at *Pockets* hope that *My Journal* helps your children establish practices that will enable them to know and claim God's presence in their daily lives.

January

Week 1

God said, "A new heart I will give you, and a new spirit I will put within you."
(Ezekiel 36:26)

"If anyone is in Christ, there is a new creation: everything old has passed away; see, everything has become new!" (2 Corinthians 5:17)

Hi! My name is Pockets. All through the year my friend Capp and I will be asking you lots of questions. We'll be writing about them in our journals, too!

It is a brand new year! What are the things you hope to do in the new year? Will you do anything differently than you did during the past year? Write here about those things:

My name is Capp. People call me that because I have 87 different caps! Pockets and I are glad we can take time away from *Pockets* magazine to be with you in your very own journal.

Write here about how you hope the world or your own community might be different by the end of this year:

People I want to pray for this week:

Prayer: Dear God, thank you for new beginnings! Amen.

January
Week 2

Read the story of Noah in your Bible. You can find it in Genesis 6:9-9:17. What do you think Noah's neighbors must have thought when they saw him building this big boat on dry land? Do you think they laughed at him? Do you think Noah was brave to do what God told him to do?

Have people ever laughed at you because you were trying to be the kind of person God wants you to be? If that has happened to you, write about how you felt. If it has never happened to you, write about how you think you would feel if that happened.

If people were laughing at one of your friends for trying to be a good person, what would you do? Write about that here, too.

Color a rainbow here to remind you of God's promise to Noah. Remember, the colors, starting at the top, are red, orange, yellow, green, blue, indigo (a very dark blue, almost purple), and violet.

People I want to pray for this week:

Prayer: Thank you, God, for the animals on the ark. Amen.

Special prayer this week: Pray for all the animals in God's creation. Pray that people everywhere will want to help God's creation.

January

Week 3

"I will sing of your steadfast love, O LORD, forever; with my mouth I will proclaim your faithfulness to all generations." (Psalm 89:1)

"Ask, and it will be given you; search, and you will find." (Matthew 7:7)

Look back at what you wrote the first week. Have you been trying to do the different thing you wrote about? Has it been hard or easy? It has probably been both hard and easy. Write about what has been hard and what has been easy.

Jesus said that what we need to do when something is hard for us is to ask for God's help. In the space below, write a letter to God, telling about the trouble you are having. Ask God to help you.

People I want to pray for this week:

Prayer: You've promised to be with me always. Knowing that makes me feel good. Thanks, God. Amen.

January

Week 4

The Old Testament has a story about a Jewish woman who had to do a very brave thing to save her people. Her name was Esther, and you can read about her in the Old Testament book named after her: the Book of Esther. Esther had become queen of Assyria, but she was still very afraid to approach the king to ask him to spare her people. When she told her uncle that she was afraid, he said something very important to her:

"Who knows? — maybe it was for a time like this that you were made queen!" (4:14, TEV

Her uncle was telling her that perhaps God had a purpose to work out through Queen Esther and that maybe that's why Esther had been made queen in the first place! Read 4:16 to find out Esther's answer. What do you think you would have done if you had been Esther?

Wow! Was Esther brave, or what! God probably doesn't want us to do anything as huge as saving a whole group of people, but God does want us to make right choices. Sometimes, we might have to be brave — like when we tell our good friend we aren't going to shoplift and that maybe he shouldn't be part of a club that made him shoplift to become a member. Write about a time when you had to do something that took a lot of courage because you knew that was what God wanted you to do.

Do you know someone who is having a hard time doing what God wants them to do? Pray for that person this week.

Prayer: Dear God, help me to know what you want me to do. Then please help me to do it. Amen.

February

Week 1

"There is nothing in all creation that will ever be able to separate us from the love of God which is ours through Jesus Christ our Lord." (Romans 8:39, TEV)

Have you ever heard this verse? Just think — it says NOTHING can separate us from God's love. ♥ No matter where we are, ♥ no matter what we do, ♥ no matter who we're with, ♥ no matter what we're thinking—God loves us!

List all of the things you are going to do or have done today. After each one, draw a heart to show that God loves you while you are doing that.

List all the places you will be or have been today. Beside each one draw a heart to show that God loves you while you are there.

List all the people you will be with or were with today. Beside each one draw a heart to show that God loves you while you are with that person. How does it make you feel to know that God always loves you?

Even when we do something that makes God unhappy, God *still* loves us! Choose a color that is a happy color for you and fill in this happy message:

GOD LOVES US!

My list:

People I want to pray for this week:

Prayer: Dear God, thank you for loving me. Help me to know how you want me to live. Amen.

February
Week 2

Jesus said, "If you love me, you will keep my commandments" (John 14:15) and "Love one another as I have loved you" (John 15:12).

When Jesus said these things to his disciples, he was telling them that we have to do more than say, "I love Jesus," and "I love God." Our actions need to show that we are loving people.

Think about the things you've done and the people you've been with over the past two or three days. Write here about which of your actions and words showed that you were a loving person.

Did you do or say something that wasn't very loving? Is there something you can do to make it better? Write down the unloving thing you did here and what you think you could do to make it better.

People I want to pray for this week:

Prayer: Dear God, help me to say loving things and do loving deeds. And when I'm not loving, God, please give me the courage to say, "I'm sorry." In Jesus' name. Amen.

February

Week 3

"Beloved, since God loved us so much, we also ought to love one another."

"Those who say, 'I love God,' and hate their brothers or sisters, are liars; for those who do not love a brother or sister whom they have seen, cannot love God whom they have not seen."

(1 John 4:11, 20)

Brothers and *sisters* here doesn't mean just our brothers and sisters in our families. It means boys and girls, men and women everywhere. What do you think the world would be like if everyone who says he or she loves God loved all people?

Is there someone or a group of people you have trouble loving? Write about the trouble you are having.

People I want to pray for this week: Pray for the person or people you are having trouble loving.

Prayer: Dear God, please help me to be more loving. Amen.

Special prayer: Ask God to help you love the person or people you are having trouble loving.

LIBRARY
St. Mark's UM Church
100 N. Highway 46 Bypass
Bloomington, IN 47408

February

Week 4

Jesus said, "'You shall love the Lord your God with all your heart, and with all your soul, and with all your mind.' This is the greatest and first commandment. And a second is like it: 'You shall love your neighbor as yourself.'" (Matthew 22:37-39)

This commandment, which Jesus said was the most important commandment, means that you have to love God in all parts of your life. You can't love God when you're in church but not love God when you're in school. You can't love God while you're working on a hunger project and not remember God when you're trying to decide how to spend your allowance.

Think about all the places you went, all the people you saw, all the things you did last week. Did you do the things God would want you to do? Did you treat others the way God would want you to treat them?

Write about your thoughts here:

Sometimes it takes courage to do or say what God want us to do or say. Do you know of a time today or during the next week when you might have trouble doing or saying what God wants? Write about that time here and ask God to help you.

People I want to pray for this week:

Something to do: Write this week's verse on an index card or a sheet of paper. Put it some place in your room where you'll see it every morning when you get out of bed.

Prayer: Dear God, I want to love you with all my heart, soul, and mind. Please help me to do that. Amen.

March
Week 1

Jesus taught by telling parables. Parables are short stories that make one main point. Jesus' parables teach us about how God wants us to live.

Read the Parable of the Unforgiving Servant in Matthew 18:23-34. Jesus tells this story to teach us that since God forgives us we ought to forgive others.

Is there someone you're having trouble forgiving for something they have done to you? Write about how you feel and why you haven't been able to forgive that person.

Sometimes it is hard to ask other people to forgive us. Write here about a time when you had to ask someone to forgive you. How did it make you feel? Was it hard to ask for forgiveness? Did the person forgive you?

People I want to pray for this week:

Prayer: Forgiving God, help me to be a forgiving person. Please give me the courage to ask for forgiveness when I have hurt someone. In Jesus' name I pray. Amen.

March
Week 2

Read the Parable of the Rich Fool in Luke 12:13-21.

Pretend you are the wealthy man in the parable. How would you finish verse 17: "He thought to himself, . . ."?

What do you think it means to be "rich toward God"?

Make a list of the possessions you have here:

What do you think it means to be "rich toward God" with your possessions?

Something special to do: This week falls during the time of year called Lent. It is the time of year when we get ready for Easter. Some people give up something special for Lent. Other people do something special for others. What is one thing you can do during Lent to get yourself ready for Easter?

_____

_____

People I want to pray for this week:

Prayer: Dear God, help me to show my love for you in the way I use my possessions. Amen.

March
Week 3

Read the Parable of the Mustard Seed and the Parable of the Yeast (Matthew 13:31-33). In these two parables Jesus talks about how very small things (the mustard seed and the yeast) can result in something very big and very important.

Close your eyes for a minute and picture a globe of the world. Picture yourself as just a tiny speck of a person among millions and millions of people. What do the parables of the mustard seed and the yeast tell you about how important you are in helping to bring in God's kingdom?

If even the smallest acts of love and service are important, what are some of the things you can do to help bring in God's kingdom?

Draw a globe of the world here. Draw lots of stick people on the globe. Now draw yourself on the globe and circle yourself to help you remember how important you are. You might want to do this on another sheet of paper, so you can draw lots and lots of people.

People I want to pray for this week:

Prayer: Dear God, thank you for the lessons Jesus taught us in his parables. I am glad to be important to your kingdom. In Jesus' name I pray. Amen.

March

Week 4

Read the Parable of the Hidden Treasure and the Parable of the Pearl of Great Price (Matthew 13:44-45).

Can you imagine anything so wonderful that you would sell everything you have just to buy that one thing?

These two parables say that the kingdom of God is just that wonderful! What do you think God's kingdom would be like? How would people treat each other? ♦ Would some people be hungry? ♦ Would there be war? ♦ Would some people be very rich and other people be very poor?

Write what you think God's kingdom would be like:

What thing that is a good and happy thing for you could be a symbol for God's kingdom? Think of your own special symbol for God's kingdom and draw it here:

People I want to pray for this week:

Prayer: Dear God, thank you for offering us a kingdom that brings love and peace and happiness. Amen.

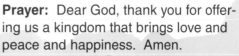

April

Week 1

Read about Jesus' resurrection in Matthew 28:1-10.

"[The women] left the tomb quickly with fear and great joy, and ran to tell his disciples [that Jesus had risen]."   (Matthew 28:8)

Easter usually comes during the month of April.* For the disciples, that first Easter was a big surprise. Jesus had died on the cross. His body had been taken down, cleaned, and wrapped in burial clothing. One of Jesus' followers was a wealthy man named Joseph of Arimathea. He had put Jesus' body in his own new tomb that had been cut out of rock. He had rolled a huge stone in front of the opening so Jesus' body would lie safely. That was the end of that, right? That's what Jesus' disciples thought. Were they going to be surprised! Can you think of a time when God surprised you with something that was really wonderful? Write about that time.

*Easter fact: Do you know how the date of Easter is figured each year? It is the first Sunday after the first full moon after the first day of spring, March 21. It can fall from March 22 through April 25.

36

How do you think Jesus' disciples felt that first Easter? How do you feel at Easter? Write about your Easter feelings here.

People I want to pray for this week:

Easter prayer: Jesus, you're alive! Hallelujah! Amen!

April

Week 2

Read about how Jesus appeared to two of his followers as they walked to Emmaus (Luke 24:13-35).

Jesus walked and talked with two of his followers, and they didn't recognize him! They even asked him to come home with them and to eat with them, and they *still* didn't recognize him! They finally realized who he was when he blessed the bread and broke it at the supper table. We don't know why they didn't recognize Jesus as they walked and talked with him. Perhaps the surprise was so great that they couldn't understand what they were seeing and hearing. After all, Jesus was dead — wasn't he? He couldn't be walking and talking with them — could he?

We see and hear Jesus in a different way today. We "see" Jesus in people who do loving things for others or who bravely stay true to their faith even when people threaten or laugh at them. Have you "seen" Jesus in another person? Write about that person here:

We "hear" Jesus when we pray and listen for what God wants us to do. Can you think of a time when you asked God to help you to know how to treat someone? If you have, write about that time and tell how God helped you. If you haven't, maybe you need help with how to treat someone now. If so, write about that.

People I want to pray for this week:

Prayer: Dear God, help me to recognize Jesus in the people around me. Please help me to take time to listen for what you want me to do. In Jesus' name I pray. Amen.

April

Week 3

Read about Jesus' resurrection in Luke 24:1-5.

"Why do you look for the living among the dead? He is not here, but has risen."

(Luke 24:5)

Jesus' disciples were sort of "stuck" in the past. Their minds couldn't take in the new things that were happening around them. That can happen to us, too. Sometimes we get "stuck" in our past. Often there is a good reason for that. We miss a friend who has moved away, or we miss the home we had before we moved. Someone we love may have become seriously ill or perhaps may have died. Our parents may have separated or divorced, so our family and home aren't the way they used to be. God is able to do new and good things for us even when these bad things happen. But sometimes we get "stuck," and we are unable to see what God is doing.

Has there been a change in your life that feels like a bad change? Write about that change here:

Do you think God might be doing something good in your life even though the change feels bad? What good things have been happening to you?

People I want to pray for this week:

Prayer: Loving God, thank you for being with me during the sad times. I am glad that you did a new and good thing for the world when you raised Jesus from the dead. Thank you for doing new and good things in my life. In Jesus' name I pray. Amen.

April

"God so loved the world that he gave his only Son, so that everyone who believes in him may not perish but have eternal life."   (John 3:16)

Write your own name on the blank line:

God loved _____ so much that he gave his only Son . . . so that

_____ will have eternal life.

Can you think of a time when you felt absolutely, without a doubt, 100 percent sure that God loves you? Write about that time here:

Do you know someone who needs to know without a doubt that God loves him or her? Ask yourself, "How can I help that person know about God's love?"

People I want to pray for this week:

Prayer: Loving God, thank you for sending Jesus to tell us about your love. Help me to show others your love by the things I say and do. Amen.

Special prayer: Pray especially for the person you named who needs to know God's love.

May
Week 1

Read about Jesus as a child in Luke 2:39-52.

"[Jesus] grew and became strong, filled with wisdom; and the favor of God was upon him."   (Luke 2:40)

"When [Jesus'] parents saw him . . . his mother said to him, 'Child, why have you treated us like this? Look, your father and I have been searching for you in great anxiety.'"   (Luke 2:48)

"[Jesus] went down with [his parents] . . . and was obedient to them." (Luke 2:51)

Sometimes we forget that Jesus was once six years old, eight years old, 10 years old. . . . The Bible doesn't tell us much about Jesus as a child. In fact, everything we know is in Luke 2. But we do know enough to know that Jesus was part of a family. We know that Mary and Joseph loved him and worried about him. We know that they taught him to love God and encouraged him to do God's will. Write a short paragraph describing your family. Tell one special thing about each person in your family.

What do you and your family do to help each other know more about God?

Write the birthdays of your family members here:

People I want to pray for this week:

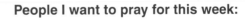

Prayer: Dear God, thank you for my family. Help us to treat each other lovingly. In Jesus' name I pray. Amen.

May
Week 2

"How very good and pleasant it is when kindred live together in unity!"

(Psalm 133:1)

Is there someone in your family whom you have a hard time getting along with? It might be a family member who lives in the same house with you, or it might be a relative who doesn't live with you. Write about the problem you have with that person. What could you do that would help you and that person to get along better together?

Write a short prayer asking God to help you and that person to treat each other lovingly. Pray your prayer every day this week.

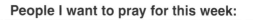

People I want to pray for this week:

Prayer: Loving God, thank you for understanding that it is hard for me to get along with some people. Help me to remember that you love both them and me. Help me to love them. Amen.

May
Week 3

Read Mark 3:31-35.
Jesus said, "Whoever does the will of God is my brother and sister and mother."
(Mark 3:35)

What strange verses these are! When we first read them, we might think that Jesus isn't being very nice to his family. But Jesus is using his family's visit as a way of making a very important point: His family includes many more people than his parents and brothers and sisters. It includes everyone who tries to do God's will. That means us!

How does it make you feel to be called a member of Jesus' family?
Name some people who are not kin to you but are part of your family because they try to do God's will.

If you want to, try to list *all* of the people you know who are part of your family because both you and they try to do God's will. You might need an extra sheet of paper to do this!

People I want to pray for this week:

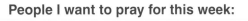

Prayer: Dear Jesus, help me to remember that we are all part of your family. Thank you for loving us. In your name I pray. Amen.

May
Week 4

"In Christ Jesus you are all children of God through faith. . . . There is no longer Jew or Greek, there is no longer slave or free, there is no longer male and female; for all of you are one in Christ Jesus."   (Galatians 3:26, 28)

No matter who we are, we are *all* God's children. That makes us all part of God's family. Think of the ways you might tell somebody else who or what you are. Are you boy or girl? Student? Soccer player or swimmer? Lover of books or lover of music? Son or daughter? Sister or brother? Niece or nephew? Caretaker for a pet? Blue-eyed person or brown-eyed person? Tall person or short person? There are probably lots more. Write the things you think of here:

Whoever I am, whatever I am, I am part of God's family.
Knowing that we are all God's children and so part of one big family can make us see people differently. Name some people or kinds of people who are part of your family because they are part of God's big family. After each name write: Welcome to my family!

Think of someone you have trouble liking. Put that person's name in the sentence below.

Whoever _____ is, whatever

_____ is, _____ is part

of God's family.

How does thinking about that person as part of your family make you feel about that person?

People I want to pray for this week:

Prayer: O God who created us all, I am glad that I am part of your family. Help me to remember that others are members of your family, too. Amen.

Read the story of Creation in Genesis 1:1-2:3.

"God saw everything that he had made, and indeed, it was very good."

(Genesis 1:31)

Just think about everything God created. There are so many different things that we can't even imagine them! What an amazing God! And what a wonderful creation! Think about the many different kinds of birds and fish and animals and trees and flowers and reptiles and vegetables and fruits and snowflakes and stars and insects. And think about all the colors. How did God think up periwinkle blue and carmine red and chartreuse green and aquamarine? And all the different kinds of people! How did you do that, God?

Write a letter to God about what you think is the best thing about creation.

Dear God,

Think about some of the people you know who are trying to take care of God's creation. What kinds of things are they doing?

What are your three favorite colors in your largest box of crayons? Make a mark with each of them here:

People I want to pray for this week:

Prayer: O God, you have created such a beautiful world. Thank you. Amen.

June
Week 2

"O Lᴏʀᴅ, how manifold are your works! In wisdom you have made them all; the earth is full of your creatures. Yonder is the sea, great and wide, creeping things innumerable are there, living things both small and great."   (Psalm 104:24-25)

Write about your favorite animal. What does it look like? Why is it your favorite? Tell God thank you for creating such a wonderful animal.

Is there something you can do — even just a very small thing — to make the world a safer place for animals? Write what you can do here:

Draw a picture of your favorite animal here:

People and animals I want to pray for this month:

Prayer: Dear God, thank you for creating so many wonderful animals. Help me to treat the animals in my neighborhood kindly. Show me ways I can help to save some of the animals that are in danger of becoming extinct.* Amen.

*When an animal becomes extinct, there are no more of that kind of animal left on the earth.

"LORD, you are the one who put me together inside my mother's body, and I praise you because of the wonderful way you created me. Everything you do is marvelous! Of this I have no doubt." (Psalm 139:13-14, CEV)

How does it make you feel to know that God created every part of you? Write about your feelings here:

All of us have something about ourselves that we don't like. Maybe our nose is too big, or maybe we have to wear glasses or braces or a hearing aid. Or maybe our hair is too curly or too straight or the "wrong" color, or we weigh too much or not enough, or we're bad at math or can't write poems, or we can't sing, or we can't play soccer well. You see, EVERYBODY has something about themselves that they don't like. But God loves us just the way we are!

Think about the things about yourself that you don't like. Make a list of them below. After each one, write "God likes the me I am."

Sometimes there are things we *do* need to change about ourselves because we are doing things that harm our bodies. Is there something you need to do to take better care of your body? Write about that thing here:

People I want to pray for this week:

Prayer: Thank you, God, for creating me to be just who I am. Help me to remember that you created each person to be special. Help me to treat every person I meet as your special creation. Amen.

June

Week 4

God said, "Every wild animal of the forest is mine, the cattle on a thousand hills. I know all the birds of the air, and all that moves in the field is mine . . . . For the world and all that is in it is mine." (Psalm 50:10-12)

Before you write in your journal this week, take a creation walk. You might walk in your backyard or your neighborhood (if that's okay with your parents), or you could ask your parents to take you to the park or to the zoo or to walk with you down your city's streets. Pay close attention to the things around you as you walk. When you have returned from your walk, list as many things as you can that you saw.

Now write about one special part of God's creation that you saw.
Did you see people misusing or abusing God's creation? Write about what you saw.

If you walk in a town or city, you may see lots of things that you usually don't think of as God's creation. But just think — who created the materials that sidewalks, buildings, and automobiles are made from? Who created people who could discover how to put those things together?

Things in God's creation that I want to pray for this week:

Prayer: Creator God, help me to be a faithful keeper of your creation. Amen.

July

Week 1

There are varieties of gifts, but the same Spirit; and there are varieties of services, but the same Lord; and there are varieties of activities, but it is the same God who activates all of them in everyone." (1 Corinthians 12:4)

What gifts or special abilities has God given you? List some of those here:

Write here about how you can use one of the gifts you just named to help other people:

Something to do: Today, try to notice the gifts of the people around you. Is someone good at making other people feel comfortable? Is someone good at making people laugh? Is someone good at explaining things that are hard to understand? If you want to, write notes to some of the people whose gifts you have noticed, saying, "Thank you for your gift of (name the gift)."

People I want to pray for this week:

Prayer: God of many gifts, thank you for the gifts you have given me. Help me to notice and give thanks for the gifts of other people, too. Amen.

"The fruit of the Spirit is love, joy, peace, patience, kindness, generosity, faithfulness, gentleness, and self-control."   (Galatians 5:22-23)

Reread the list above. Do you have the fruit of the spirit? Write about how you see these "fruits" in yourself. (For example, how do you show love and joy? When are you patient? Are you gentle when you speak and act? Do you control your behavior so that you don't act in ways that would not be pleasing to God?)

Are there any of the things listed in the scripture passage that you need to work on? Write here about one of the "fruits" that you want to improve on.

People I want to pray for this week:

Prayer: Loving God, I hope that other people see the fruit of your Spirit in me. Help me to show that fruit to everyone. Amen.

July
Week 3

"Once you were darkness, but now in the Lord you are light. Live as children of light."
(Ephesians 5:8)

Think for a minute about light. Think about sunlight, candles, campfires, fireflies, stars, lamps, flashlights, and any other kind of light you can think of. How does light make people feel? What does it mean to live as "children of light"?

Write about how you can be light for someone you know.

Write about one way you can be light for your community or even the world.

People I want to pray for this week:

Something to do: Make a poster showing your favorite kind of light, and write the words "Live as children of light" on it.

Prayer: Dear God, help me to live as a child of the light, showing your love to everyone I meet. Amen.

"I thank my God every time I remember you, constantly praying with joy in every one of my prayers for all of you."   (Philippians 1:3-4

In his letters to his friends in the early churches, Paul often reminded the Christians in those churches that he was praying for them. It's important to pray for the people we love.

Who are the people you pray for? What kind of things do you ask God when you are praying for the people you love? Do you pray for people you've never met? What are some of the things you ask God when you are praying for people you don't know?

Do you know who some of the people are who pray for you? Write here about who those people are and why they pray for you.

People I want to pray for this week:

Prayer: Loving God, thank you for always hearing our prayers. Thank you for the people who pray for me and the people for whom I pray. Amen.

August

Week 1

"Be doers of the words, and not merely hearers who deceive themselves."

(James 1:22)

This scripture says it's not enough simply to read our Bibles. We also have to do what God tells us to do. Write here about some of the things that God tells us to do that are really hard for you.

Write here about how you can begin to be a doer of one of the things that you wrote about that is hard for you.

People I want to pray for this week:

Prayer: Gracious God, you know that sometimes it's hard for me to do what I know you want me to do. Give me courage to be a doer of your word. Amen.

M·HAVERFIELD·

"No one can tame the tongue—a restless evil, full of deadly poison. With it we bless the Lord . . . and with it we curse those who are made in the likeness of God. . . . My brothers and sisters, this ought not to be so." (James 3:8-10)

James says that it is not right for those who love God to say bad things about other people. Can you think of a time when something you said hurt someone? Write here about what happened and what you learned from the experience:

Now write about a time when you were hurt by something someone else said. What happened? What did you learn from the experience?

People I want to pray for this week:

Prayer: Loving God, help me to remember you before I speak. When my words have hurt someone, give me the courage to ask for forgiveness. Amen.

M·HAVERFIELD·

August

Week 3

"The prayer of the righteous is powerful and effective."   (James 5:16)

Can you think of a time when you knew for sure that God had answered one of your prayers? Write about that time here:

Can you think of a time when one of your prayers didn't seem to be answered? How did you feel? Did you keep praying?

Write about a time when God answered one of your prayers in a way that was completely different from what you expected.

People I want to pray for this week:

Prayer: Loving God, sometimes I don't understand when I don't see the answer I expected to my prayers, but I know that you always hear me and always want the best for all your children. Thank you, God, for always listening to me. Amen.

M·HAVERFIELD·

August

Week 4

"Once you were not a people, but now you are God's people; once you had not received mercy, but now you have received mercy." (1 Peter 2:10)

We know that, like the scripture says, we are God's people. How does that make a difference in the way we treat other people? Write here about what difference being one of God's people makes in your life.

What does it mean to show mercy? If you don't know what *mercy* means, look it up. Then write about how you have received mercy and how you have shown mercy to someone else.

Something to do: Make a list of all the words you can think of that describe how God's people act. Do those words describe how you act?

_____

_____

_____

_____

_____

_____

_____

People I want to pray for this week:

Prayer: Merciful God, help me to remember that being one of your people is the most important thing that I can be. Forgive me when I forget to act like one of your people. Amen.

·M·HAVERFIELD·

September
Week 1

Moses said to God, "Who am I that I should go to Pharaoh, and bring the Israelites out of Egypt?"
(Exodus 3:11)

Have you ever felt like God wanted you to do something you weren't sure you could do? Did you do it? If so, what helped you to be able to do it? Did you learn anything?

If you didn't do what you felt like God wanted you to, what would have helped you to be able to do it? Did you wish you had done what you felt God wanted you to do? Did you learn anything?

People I want to pray for this week:

Prayer: God, sometimes it's really hard for me to do the things I know you want me to do. Help me to know what you want me to do and give me the courage to do it. Amen.

September

Week 2

"The time that the Israelites had lived in Egypt was four hundred thirty years. At the end of four hundred thirty years, on that very day, all the companies of the LORD went out from Egypt."

(Exodus 12: 40-41)

The Israelites had been treated badly in Egypt, but they had lived there for many years. How do you think they felt when they left? Pretend you are one of the children whose family left Egypt in the Exodus. Write here about how you are feeling as your family leaves:

Is there someone new in your class or school this year? How do you think that person might feel right now? Write here about some ways you can make someone who is new to your school feel welcome.

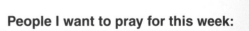

People I want to pray for this week:

Prayer: Loving God, sometimes what lies ahead of me seems scary, but I know that you are always with me. That helps me go on even when I feel nervous or afraid. Thank you for helping me through those times. Amen.

September

Week 3

Ruth said, "Do not press me to leave you or to turn back from following you! Where you go, I will go." (Ruth 1:16)

Read chapter 1 of the Book of Ruth. By choosing to go with Naomi, Ruth was giving up her home, the life she had always known, and, probably, the chance to marry again and have children. Who are the people who love you enough to stick with you no matter what? Write here about those people:

Who are the people that you love enough to stick with no matter what? Write here about why you would always stick with those people.

People I want to pray for this week:

Prayer: Steadfast God, thank you for the people in our lives who always love us and always stand by us. They help us to remember what your love for us is like. Amen.

81

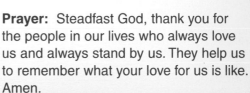

September

Week 4

"Let all that you do be done in love."   (1 Corinthians 16:14)

It's hard to do everything in a loving way. Write here about a time in the last week when you have acted in a way that was not loving. Write as much as you can remember about what you did and why you did it.

Write about what you could have done differently in the situation you just wrote about to act in a way that was loving.

People I want to pray for this week:

Something to do: Make a card for yourself with the verse from 1 Corinthians. Color or decorate it any way you want. Put it in a place where you will see it often, such as on your bedroom mirror or the back of your door; or put the card in your backpack and carry it with you. When you see the card, it will remind you of how God wants us to act.

Prayer: God, your way is the loving way! Help me to remember that and to treat others with love so that they can see your love in me. Amen.

October

"Can a woman forget her nursing child, or show no compassion for the child of her womb? Even these may forget, yet I will not forget you."   (Isaiah 49:15)

Do you think your parents would ever forget you? No way! But God says even if our parents did forget us, God would never forget us. Write here about how it feels to be remembered always by God.

Even though we know God will never forget us, did you ever have a time when you felt like God might have forgotten about you or didn't care about you? Write here about that time and about what helped you to know that God really did remember you and love you.

People I want to pray for this week:

Something to do: Cut a narrow strip of construction paper and write on it "God will never forget you!" Decorate it any way you want. Give it to someone you know who might be feeling discouraged to use as a bookmark.

Prayer: Loving God, thank you for always remembering me and always loving me! Amen.

October

Week 2

"The word that came to Jeremiah from the Lord: Stand in the gate of the Lord's house, and proclaim there this word. . . . Amend your ways and your doings."

(Jeremiah 7:1-3)

Prophets like Jeremiah sometimes had to tell people really hard things. These were things that were true but that the people didn't want to hear. Have you ever had to tell somebody something really hard? What made it hard to tell? How did the person you had to tell act when you told him or her?

Now think about a time when someone told you something that was true but that you really didn't want to hear. What did the person tell you? Why didn't you want to hear? How did you act when the person told you?

People I want to pray for this week:

Prayer: Dear God, sometimes it's really hard to tell someone a truth that they need to hear. Give me courage to tell the truth, and help me to open my ears when someone has to tell me a hard truth. Amen.

October

Week 3

"Although Daniel knew that the document had been signed, he continued to go to his house, which had windows in its upper room open toward Jerusalem, and to get down on his knees three times a day to pray to his God and praise him, just as he had done previously."

(Daniel 6:10)

King Darius had signed a law making it illegal for people to pray, except to him. The punishment for breaking the law was to be thrown into a den of hungry lions. Daniel knew about the law, but he continued to pray three times a day. Have you ever had to stand up for what you believe in the way Daniel did, even though you knew it might cause problems for you? Write here about a time you had to stand up for your beliefs:

Has there ever been a time when you wanted to stand up for something you believed in but didn't? If you've ever had a time like that, write about it here. Write about what happened, why you didn't stand up for your beliefs, and what you wish you might have done differently.

People I want to pray for this week:

Prayer: God, help me to be brave enough to stand up for what I know is right, even when it might get me into trouble or cause me to be laughed at by my friends. Amen.

October

Week 4

"What does the LORD require of you but to do justice, and to love kindness, and to walk humbly with your God?"
(Micah 6:8)

Look up the word *justice* in a dictionary and talk to a few people about what they think the word means. Then think about some ways that you could "do justice" in your home or neighborhood or school. List four or five of those things below.

Pick one of the things that you wrote about in the first question and write down any steps you need to take to do it. Then write about how doing that will make things more just or fair.

People I want to pray for this week:

Something to do: Read the newspapers or watch the news on television and notice stories about people being treated unjustly. Pray for those people.

Prayer: Dear God, I want to work to help make the world a more just place. Help me to see the places where injustice exists around me and show me how I can work for justice. Amen.

November

Week 1

"I have heard of your faith in the Lord Jesus and your love toward all the saints, and for this reason I do not cease to give thanks for you as I remember you in my prayers." (Ephesians 1:15-16)

November 1 is All Saints' Day. On All Saints' Day we honor the saints who have been important in the history of the church and people living now who try to follow God's ways. Think about the people you know in your community, school, church, and even in your family. Write here about one or two people who are saints of God.

Now think about the ways in which you are a saint. Write here about something you have done that showed that you are a saint of God.

People I want to pray for this week:

Something to do: This week try to notice whenever someone in your family does something kind for someone else. Write these things down. At the end of the week, tell your family members what you noticed.

Prayer: Dear God, thank you for all the saints who have shown us how to love and serve you. Help me to be one of your saints. Amen.

November

Week 2

"Praise the LORD! Sing to the LORD a new song, his praise in the assembly of the faithful." (Psalm 149:1)

What things make you feel like praising God? Make a list here of some of the things that make you feel most like praising God:

Write your own psalm or poem of praise to God. Mention some of the things you listed above and write about how those things make you feel.

People I want to pray for this week:

Prayer: Wonderful God, it is good to give praise to you because you have created us and you love us always. Amen.

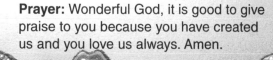

November

Week 3

"Turn to me and be gracious to me, for I am lonely and afflicted. Relieve the troubles of my heart, and bring me out of my distress."   (Psalm 25:16-17)

In this psalm, instead of offering a prayer of praise, the writer was asking God for something. We call that a prayer of petition. How do you think the person who wrote this prayer was feeling? Write about a time when you felt that way and about how God helped you.

Now write your own psalm or prayer of petition to God. You don't have to be asking God for the things the writer of Psalm 25 was asking for. Your psalm can be about anything you want to ask of God.

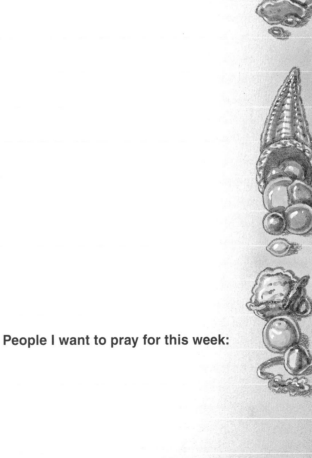

People I want to pray for this week:

Prayer: Gracious God, thank you for your comforting love when I feel sad and lonely. Amen.

November

Week 4

"You visit the earth and water it, you greatly enrich it; the river of God is full of water; you provide the people with grain, for so you have prepared it."   (Psalm 65:9

Some of the psalms, like this one, are praising God for the wonders of God's creation and for providing for the people. Think for a minute about God's creation. What are some of the things about God's creation that make you feel most thankful? Write about those below.

Now write a psalm giving thanks for how wonderful God's creation is. Make your psalm full of joy.

People I want to pray for this week:

Something to do: If you want to, you can read the psalms you've written this month with your family, maybe at your Thanksgiving dinner or at another family meal.

Prayer: God, your creation is beautiful and marvelous. Help us to take care of what you have created. Amen.

December

Week 1

"Be patient, therefore, beloved, until the coming of the Lord."   (James 5:7)

The people of Israel had waited a very long time for their Messiah to come. Write here about a time when you had to wait a long time for something. Was it hard to wait? When what you were waiting for finally came, did it seem worth waiting for?

What can you do while you're waiting? Write here about the things you can do to make waiting easier.

Do you think God is waiting for anything? Write about what you think God might be waiting for.

People I want to pray for this month:

Prayer: Dear God, you know how hard it is for me to wait. Help me learn to wait patiently for the good things you have in store for me. Amen.

December

Week 2

"This is my prayer, that your love may overflow more and more with knowledge and full insight to help you to determine what is best, so that in the day of Christ you may be pure and blameless, having produced the harvest of righteousness that comes through Jesus Christ for the glory and praise of God."　　　　　(Philippians 1:9-11)

Your family is probably doing lots of things to get ready for Christmas. Write here about the things you and your family are doing to help you know that it is Jesus' birthday you are getting ready for.

Pick one of the things you wrote about that is special or really important to you. What makes it special? How would you feel if you didn't get to do that thing this year?

People I want to pray for this week:

Prayer: Loving God, we are all getting ready to celebrate Christmas. It's a busy, exciting time. But you know that sometimes we get so busy we almost forget what we're celebrating. Help us to remember. Amen.

December

Week 3

Read Mary's Song in Luke 1:46-55.

How do you think Mary felt when she first found out that God had chosen her to be Jesus' mother? How would you feel if God asked you to do something very important that other people might not understand? Write here about how you think Mary felt and how you might feel.

Even though Mary might have been scared or nervous or confused, she said "Yes" to God's plan because she trusted God. Is it easy for you to trust God? What makes it easy or hard?

People I want to pray for this month:

Prayer: Gracious God, I want to trust you the way Mary did. Help me to trust you so that I can do what you want me to do. Amen.

December

Week 4

The angel said, . . . "Do not be afraid; for see—I am bringing you good news of great joy for all the people: to you is born this day in the city of David a Savior, who is the Messiah, the Lord." (Luke 2:10-11)

Pretend you are one of the shepherds who was out in the fields that first Christmas night. Write about what it might have been like and how you felt.

Write here about ways you can share the joy of Christmas with someone you know who may be lonely or discouraged.

People I want to pray for this week:

Prayer: God of Christmas surprises, thank you for Jesus, the greatest gift of all! Amen.

"You shall have no other gods before me."   (Exodus 20:3)

This verse is the first of the Ten Commandments. It's really easy to keep that commandment, isn't it? After all, do we know anyone who worships idols? Probably not! But the words *before me* are a little tricky. It is easy to let something become so important in our lives that we put it before worshiping God — things like having lots of money or being popular or being a good athlete or having the newest clothes.

Is there something so important to you that it has become (or might become) more important to you than God? Write it here:

Tell why that thing is so important to you.

People I want to pray for this week:

Prayer: Loving God, help me to keep you the most important thing in my life. Amen.

Spring

Read Matthew 16:1-4.

The religious leaders in Jesus' time asked Jesus for a sign from heaven. They were testing him to see if he really had been sent by God. Jesus told them that the signs of God's activity were all around them, but they were so busy looking for miracles that they didn't see the signs.

Signs of God's presence in our lives are everywhere — in the lives of good people and in the new life of spring. What person is a sign of God's presence in your life?

What are some of the signs of spring that you see around you this week?

People I want to pray for this week:

Prayer: O God who creates, help me to be a sign of your presence in someone's life. In Jesus' name. Amen.

109

"Happy are those that work for peace; God will call them his children!"

(Matthew 5:9, TEV)

Here are some ways Jesus said we could be peacemakers: ♥ feed the hungry, give water to the thirsty, give clothes to those who have no clothes (Matthew 25:31-40) ♥ love and pray for our enemies (Matthew 25:31-40) ♥ do not take more than we need (Matthew 6:19) ♥ do not judge others (Matthew 7:1) ♥ love one another (John 15:16). Look at the ways Jesus taught us to be peacemakers. What are some of the ways you try to do some of these things?

Draw a picture of something that for you is a peaceful thing.

People I want to pray for this week:

Prayer: Dear Jesus, help me to be a peacemaker. Help me to plant seeds of love instead of hate, seeds of light instead of darkness, seeds of joy instead of sadness. Amen.

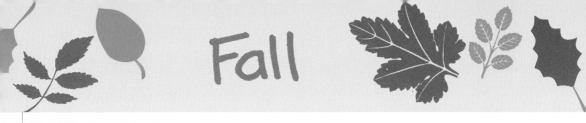

Read Matthew 18:1-5.
Jesus said, "Whoever welcomes one such child in my name welcomes me."

When we welcome people, we make them feel wanted. We make them feel comfortable. We make them feel as good as they would feel at home.
Can you think of a time when someone tried very hard to make you feel welcome? Write about that time here.

Is there someone you need to make welcome at school or Sunday school or in your neighborhood or in some other group you belong to? Write about how you can do that.

People I want to pray for this week:

Prayer: Loving God, please help me make persons around me feel welcome. Help me especially to see those people whom others have made to feel unwelcome, and give me the courage to welcome them. In Jesus' name. Amen.   111

Discover the Magazine
That Helps Your Child Grow Up Learning More About God's Love

pockets®

Unforgettable characters like me, Wendell!

Each issue brings to your home—

- "Pocketsful of Prayer"
- "Pocketsful of Scripture"
- Stories
- Journaling Pages
- Games and Activities
- Simple Recipes
- Poems
- Full-Color Art
- Unforgettable Characters

Children will . . .

GROW UP KNOWING—that God is with them
GROW UP PRAYING—as they develop their relationship with God
GROW UP READING—because POCKETS is written just for them
GROW UP FEELING APPRECIATED—confident of God's love for them

11 issues—only $16.95
Call (800) 925-6847
For children ages 6-12